THE HEART IS THE NEW BRAIN

Amazon Bestseller #1

Tulanahinaa

Booklover Publishing House

PUBLISHED BY:

BOOKLOVER PUBLISHING HOUSE, INDIA

ISBN: 978-81-974761-0-5

Second Edition: 2024

CONTENTS

THE HEART'S COUP D'ÉTAT: A COMICAL STEER TO LIFE WITH A NEW BRAIN AND OTHER RIDICULOUS DISCOVERIES

That's right folks! The heart has staged a coup and taken over as the new brain. Today, we find ourselves amidst a scientific revolution so absurd that it makes the idea of cats ruling the world seem downright sensible.

As whimsical as it may sound, we will take a lighthearted romp through the wacky implications of this topsy-turvy twist and ponder the age-old questions. Grab your sense of humor and let us dive in!

Cheers to the most outlandish scientific development since someone decided to put pineapple on pizza: The Heart is the New Brain. Yes, you read that right!

First off, let us address the rather perplexing questions:

If the heart is the new brain, does that make the spleen the new heartthrob? Or does it then make the stomach the new heart?

How did we end up in a world where the heart reigns supreme as the new brain? Did someone mix up their anatomy flashcards?

Was there a coup in the body's central command center? Or better still did the heart stage a coup while the brain was busy contemplating the nature of existence?

Did the brain go on a strike and hand over the reins to the heart in a fit of temper? Or did the brain decide it needed a sabbatical and hand over the keys?

And wait, there's more!

If the heart is the new brain, does that mean we'll have hearty debates instead of heated discussions? Or heartfelt conversations instead of heart-to-heart talks?

Will we be encouraged to follow our heartbeats instead of our trains of thought? Or will we be encouraged to wear our emotions on our sleeves, quite literally?

And what about those moments when we are told to "use our heads"? Does that phrase now hold any weight, or should we just pat our chests and hope for the best?

Are we saying one fine morning a group of scientists proclaimed, "You Heart! You are in charge now." And just like that, the heart became the CEO of the body, leaving the brain to ponder on its newfound freedom?

Well, we may never know, but one thing is for sure: The heart is now calling the shots and we are all just along for the whimsical ride. So, move over cerebral cortex – there is a new boss in town, and it is the squishy, lovey-dovey, sometimes erratic heart!

Buckle up, because we are about to embark on a journey through the absurdity of it all!

Let us talk about what this means for everyday life.

Let us delve into the practical implications of this ludicrous paradigm shift.

Picture this: Imagine a world where instead of using our heads to solve problems, we tap into the wisdom of our hearts. Clutching your chest in earnest, you tell the heart, "I need to ace this exam, so please heart, channel your inner Einstein and help me out here." Or maybe more scarily you tell the heart, "Listen up, heart, we've got a calculus exam tomorrow and I am counting on you to pull through." Then when you are taking the test and instead of furiously cramming facts, you are now expected to gaze lovingly at your textbook and hope your heart magically absorbs the information. My pragmatic child will say, "Good luck with that strategy, Mama!"

In this brave new world, we can envision a slew of heart-based job titles popping up: Heart Surgeon becomes *Brain Surgeon* or *Chief Brain Operator*, Cardiologist becomes *Cerebrologist* or *Neurologist Extraordinaire,* and Cupid becomes... well, Cupid still remains The Cupid, because you can't mess with a classic, some things are just too iconic to change.

On a more serious note, if the heart truly is taking over as the new brain, we might need to rethink our idioms and expressions. "Cold feet" could become "*cold ventricles*" and "change of heart" might transform into "*change of hypothalamus*" or *"change of medulla oblongata."* It is a linguistic minefield out there, folks!

Perhaps the brain got too big for it is own neurons and decided to outsource the responsibilities to the heart.

Whatever the case, we can't help but picture a tiny heart wearing a miniature crown and strutting around like it is the ruler of all bodily functions.

In conclusion, the idea that the heart is the new brain is as absurd as it is amusing, isn't it?

Let us dive a bit deeper into the concept...

Our brain is very good at helping us solve problems, understand new things and remember important information. It is like our own personal supercomputer! But our heart is really good at something else - it helps us understand how we FEEL.

When we are happy, our heart might feel light and bouncy and when we are sad, it might feel heavy. Our heart can tell us a lot about *how we are doing* and *what we need.*

Sometimes, when we have to make a decision or understand how someone else is feeling, don't we feel it is important to listen to our heart as well as our brain? That is what people mean when they say *heart is the new brain*. It is like saying that our feelings and emotions are just as important as our thoughts and ideas.

So, when we listen to our heart, we can understand ourselves and others better. It is like having two very important parts of ourselves working together to help us be the best person we can be.

When we think about the expression *heart is the new brain*, in the context of music, it becomes even more interesting! Music has a special way of connecting with our emotions and feelings, much like our heart does. Our brains help us understand the structure of music, like the rhythm, melody and harmony. We use our brains to learn how to play instruments and remember the words to songs.

But the really amazing thing about music is how it makes us feel. When we listen to a happy song, it can make our hearts feel light and joyful, and when we hear a sad song, it might make our hearts feel heavy with emotion.

So, in a way, music helps us understand the idea of *heart is the new brain* because it speaks to our emotions and feelings just as much as it speaks to our thoughts and understanding. When we listen to music, we are using both our brains and our hearts to connect with the music and the feelings it brings out in us.

In this way, *heart is the new brain* can be seen as a way of saying that we should pay attention to how music makes us feel, not just how we understand it. It is like music giving us a special way to use both our brains and our hearts together, helping us understand and express our emotions in a really beautiful and powerful way.

This concept encourages people to consider the wisdom and guidance that come from their emotions and intuition, not just from logical thinking. It also highlights the value of kindness, compassion and connecting with others on an emotional level.

In today's world, where there is often a strong emphasis on academic and intellectual achievements, the power of *heart is the new brain* reminds us that our emotional well-being, our ability to relate to others, and our capacity for empathy are equally important for leading a fulfilling and meaningful life.

This concept can inspire people to listen to their hearts, trust their instincts and cultivate their emotional intelligence, ultimately leading to better relationships, improved communication and a deeper understanding of themselves and the world around them.

Furthermore, the concept of heart being the new brain, can albeit be considered a futuristic idea because it challenges the traditional ways of thinking about intelligence and cognition.

Historically, intelligence has been primarily associated with cognitive abilities, such as logical reasoning, problem-solving and analytical thinking, which are functions of the brain.

However, as we continue to learn more about emotions, empathy and the interconnectedness of mind and body, there is a growing recognition of the significance of emotional intelligence and intuition.

In the future, as our understanding of neuroscience, psychology and holistic health continues to evolve, we may see a shift towards a more integrated view of intelligence - one that acknowledges the important role of emotions and the heart in decision-making, creativity and overall well-being. This could have profound implications for fields such as education, psychology and leadership, as well as determine how we approach personal development and human relationships.

Additionally, advancements in technology and artificial intelligence may also play a role in shaping this futuristic idea. As machines become increasingly proficient at tasks traditionally associated with cognitive intelligence, there may be a greater emphasis on the unique qualities of human emotional intelligence, empathy and intuition as essential aspects of what it means to be intelligent.

It is important to note that this expression is metaphorical and not a literal statement about the physiological functions of the heart and brain. Both organs have distinct roles in our bodies, with the brain being responsible for cognitive processes and the heart for pumping blood and providing oxygen to the body's cells.

And while the brain is undoubtedly essential for cognitive functions and analytical thinking, it is important to note that the heart, metaphorically representing emotions and empathy, has a profound influence on our thoughts, behavior and relationships.

Therefore, embracing emotional intelligence, understanding our emotions and those of others can lead to better decision-making, improved relationships and overall psychological well-being.

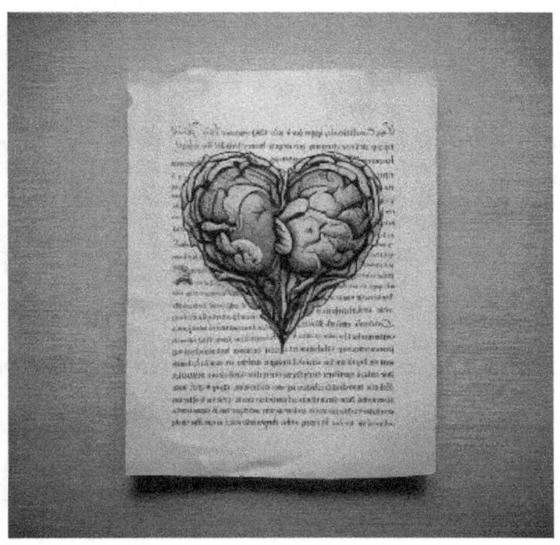

As a Human Being I am all Heart so My Heart wrote to my Brain…

Dear Brain,

I hope this message finds you well. I'm writing to share with you an intriguing concept that has been gaining traction in scientific and philosophical circles – the idea that the heart may be considered the new "brain". This fascinating concept has actually challenged my long-held beliefs about the nature of intelligence and consciousness. It appears that the heart, traditionally viewed as a mere pump, may play a far more profound role in shaping human experiences than I had ever imagined.

Recent research and studies have revealed fascinating insights into the complex and intricate functions of the heart, far beyond the traditional role as a simple pump. It turns out that the heart has its own independent nervous system, comprising around 40,000 neurons, often referred to as the "heart brain." This intricate network enables the heart to communicate with the brain and the rest of the body, influencing our perception, emotional experiences, and overall well-being in profound ways.

Furthermore, the heart produces and releases several hormones and neurotransmitters that play a crucial role in regulating emotional responses, decision-making, and cognitive functions. These findings challenge the long-held belief that the brain is the sole orchestrator of our thoughts and emotions.

This discovery actually suggests that the heart possesses its own form of intelligence, capable of influencing our emotions, perceptions and decision-making in ways that extend beyond my own domain. In fact, in the light of these discoveries, it is becoming increasingly apparent that the heart's influence extends far beyond the mechanical function of pumping blood. It seems to actively contribute to the emotional and cognitive processes, shaping our perceptions and responses to the world around us.

It is a paradigm shift that I find both captivating and humbling. And as we continue to explore and understand the intricate relationship between the heart and the brain, It is fascinating to contemplate the implications of this paradigm shift.

Do you think this new perspective might influence our approach to health, psychology and human potential?

What insights might it offer into the intricate interplay between emotion and cognition?

Could it be that the heart, with its intricate neural network and profound influence on our emotions and cognition, plays a more significant role in shaping our experiences and decisions than previously thought?

I am beginning to believe that acknowledging the heart's significance as a center of intelligence could revolutionize our understanding of human consciousness and pave the way for new approaches to health, well-being and human potential.

I look forward to hearing your thoughts on this captivating topic and engaging in a stimulating discussion about the evolving understanding of our internal workings.

Warm Regards,

The Heart

And this is what the Brain replied…

Subject: Re: The Heart as the New Brain

Dear Heart,

Thank you for bringing this thought-provoking concept to my attention. The evolving understanding of the heart's complexities and the potential significance in shaping human experiences is indeed fascinating.

As the traditional seat of intelligence and cognitive function, I have long been regarded as the primary organ responsible for processing information, regulating emotions and guiding decision-making. However, the recent findings regarding your intricate neural network and its influence on emotional and cognitive processes are undeniably thought-provoking.

It is intriguing to consider the possibility that you - the heart, with your autonomous nervous system and the capacity to influence one's perceptions and responses, may play a more substantial role in shaping human experiences than previously acknowledged.

The notion of the heart as an intelligent, perceptive organ capable of impacting our emotional and cognitive states challenges conventional perspectives on human consciousness and well-being.

For centuries, I have been regarded as the seat of intelligence and cognitive function, responsible for processing information and regulating emotions.

Yet, as I ponder the implications of your newfound significance, I can't help but feel a sense of awe at the complexity of the human body and the interconnectedness of its various systems.

I agree with you that embracing the idea of the heart as the new brain challenges the conventional understanding of human consciousness. It raises profound questions about the nature of intelligence and the mechanisms that shape our experiences.

I believe that further exploration and interdisciplinary collaboration are essential to unraveling the full extent of the heart's influence whilst understanding how it integrates with the complex network of functions that I oversee.

Further, embracing this paradigm shift could lead to new insights into human cognition, emotional regulation and overall health, therefore potentially opening doors to innovative approaches in fields ranging from psychology to medicine.

As I contemplate these questions, I am reminded of the boundless mysteries that still await our exploration!

I am eager to delve deeper into this thought-provoking topic and to explore the implications for further understanding of the human intelligence and well-being.

I welcome the opportunity to engage in meaningful discussions and collaborative endeavors as we continue to unravel the mysteries of human consciousness and the intricate interplay between the heart and the brain.

Thank you once again for sharing this thought-provoking perspective!

I can't help but feel excited to visualize that together, You and I, may yet reveal deeper truths about the human experience!!

With curiosity and anticipation,

Best Regards,

The Brain

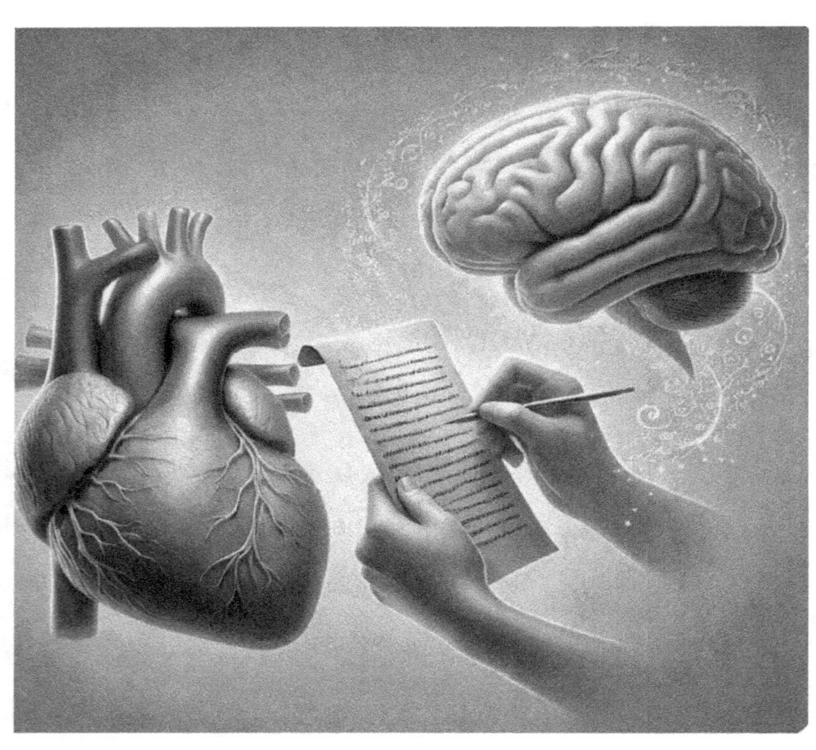

A fictitious story woven to explain the concept to my teenage child....

Story Title: Heart, the New Brain

Once upon a time in a world much like our own, there existed a society where people believed that the heart was the seat of wisdom and intelligence. In this extraordinary world, the heart was considered to be the true source of understanding, empathy and decision-making.

In the bustling city of Veritum, there lived a young woman named Elara. She possessed a remarkable ability to perceive the emotions of others and understand their unspoken thoughts. This unique talent had always set her apart from her peers and she often found herself drawn to those in need of guidance and support.

In Veritum, the Heart Council, an esteemed group of elders, were revered for their profound wisdom and insight. They were responsible for guiding the city's decisions and resolving conflicts, drawing upon the collective wisdom of their hearts.

One day, a crisis befell the city. A deep divide had emerged between two prominent districts, leading to escalating tensions and discord. The Heart Council convened to address the growing conflict, but their deliberations seemed to yield little progress. As the situation worsened, Elara felt a stirring within her own heart, urging her to take action.

Driven by a profound sense of empathy and a desire to heal the rift, Elara embarked on a journey to seek the counsel of the legendary Sage of Serenity, an enigmatic figure rumored to possess unparalleled insight into the mysteries of the heart.

Venturing through verdant forests and across sweeping plains, Elara finally arrived at the secluded sanctuary of the Sage. The Sage, a gentle and wise soul, welcomed her with warmth and understanding. Together, they delved into the depths of Elara's own heart, unlocking the dormant wisdom that lay within.

Through their shared contemplation and introspection, Elara discovered the interconnectedness of all hearts and the boundless potential for empathy and understanding. She realized that the key to resolving the conflict in Veritum lay not in logic or strategy, but in the profound empathy and compassion that resided within every individual.

Returning to the city, Elara shared her newfound insight with the people, encouraging them to listen to the whispers of their own hearts and to understand the hearts of others. As her words spread, a transformation began to take root. People from both districts, moved by the sincerity and compassion in Elara's message, started to open their hearts to one another.

Slowly but steadily, the animosity and division that had gripped the city began to dissolve. Through heartfelt conversations and acts of kindness, the people of Veritum bridged the gap that had separated them, forging bonds of empathy and understanding.

In the wake of this transformation, the Heart Council recognized the profound truth that Elara had revealed: that the heart, with it is capacity for empathy and understanding, was indeed the true seat of wisdom. From that day forward, the people of Veritum embraced a new era, where decisions were guided not by the mind alone, but by the collective wisdom and compassion of their hearts.

And so, in a world where the heart became the new brain, empathy, understanding, and compassion flourished, illuminating a path toward a future where the wisdom of the heart prevailed above all.

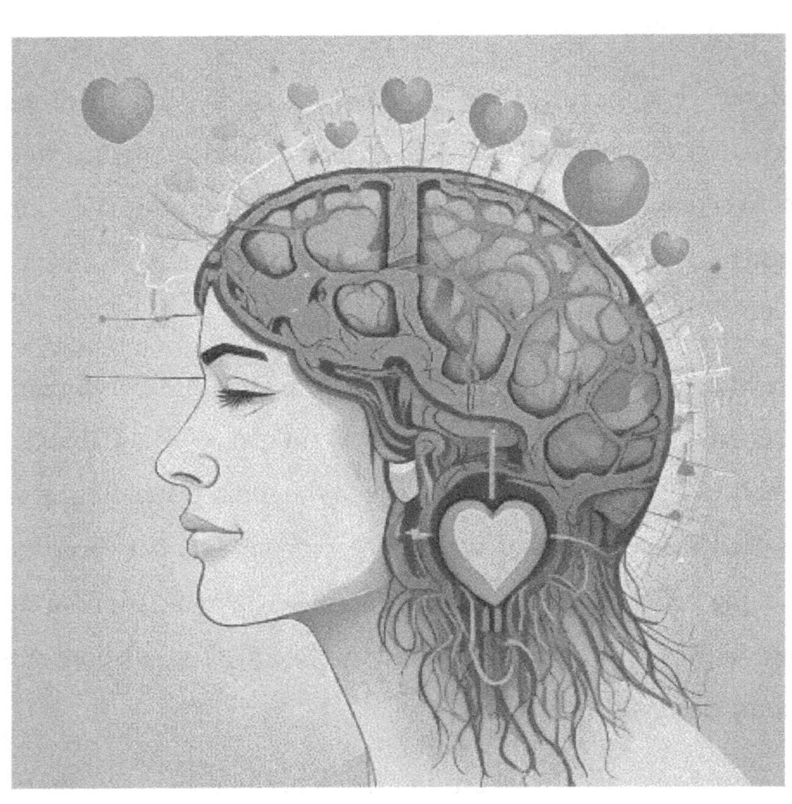

UNDERSTANDING THE NUANCES OF THE BRAIN AND THE HEART IN THE POETIC SENSE

In the realm where wisdom blooms,

A truth emerges and consumes,

Heart is the new brain, we say,

Where emotions guide and find their way.

Within the chambers deep and true,

A language spoken, old and new,

Emotional intelligence takes its course,

Guiding us with its gentle force.

Through beating rhythms, strong and clear,

The heart's wisdom begins to appear,

Intuition's whisper softly aligns,

As logic and reason interweave with the divine.

No longer confined to thoughts alone,

The heart's intelligence has clearly shown,

Those emotions, too, hold great might,

In shaping our decisions, in love's pure light.

With empathy as our guiding star,

We navigate the paths that seem afar,

Connecting souls in kind embrace,

Embracing hearts as we find our place.

In this dance of heart and brain,

A harmonious union we attain,

Balancing the ebb and flow,

Into a wisdom we come to know.

So let us honor this sacred truth,

In our lives, from our youth,

Heart is the new brain, we proclaim,

Unleashing it is power, igniting our flame.

For within our very being,

Lies the magic we are seeing,

Heart is the new brain, we say,

In love's embrace, we find our way.

THE HEART'S HOSTILE TAKEOVER:

AN ABSURD GUIDE TO THE NEW BRAIN IN TOWN

CHAPTER 1:

RETHINKING INTELLIGENCE

In this chapter, we will delve on the contemporary exploration of intelligence and challenge the traditional notions of intelligence that focus primarily on cognitive abilities and logical reasoning. And accordingly, we will expand our understanding of intelligence to incorporate emotional intelligence, intuition and the power of the heart. This paradigm advocates for a holistic understanding of intelligence by emphasizing the essential role of the heart in shaping human cognition and emotional well-being.

1.1 Expanding traditional notions of intelligence:

The conventional understanding of intelligence, has predominantly focused on cognitive abilities such as logical reasoning, problem-solving, and academic achievements. However, this narrow definition overlooks the crucial role of emotions and intuition in decision-making, creativity, and overall human experience. Although logic and rationality are valuable, there are limitations of relying solely on a logical approach. And here comes in *Emotions* which can provide important information and guidance, allowing for a more complete understanding of situations and enabling better decision-making.

I am sure you will agree that denying or suppressing emotions can lead to stress, burnout and an imbalance in our lives. Thus, intelligence which was solely a product of cognitive abilities needs a transformative shift towards a more comprehensive understanding that integrates emotional awareness, empathy and compassion as intrinsic components of

intelligence. By rethinking intelligence through the lens of the heart, we can aspire to build societies that prioritize empathy and understanding, ultimately enriching the human experience and fostering a more compassionate world. Recognizing the intricate ways in which our emotions inform our thoughts and behaviors, underscores the importance of qualities such as intuition, empathy and mindfulness as crucial aspects of a well-rounded and effective intelligence, thereby contributing to a more nuanced and human-centered understanding of the mind.

1.2 Cultivating the popular concept of Emotional Intelligence:

Emotional intelligence refers to the ability to recognize, understand, and manage our own emotions as well as understand and empathize with the emotions of others. It involves skills such as self-awareness, self-regulation, empathy and social awareness. Proponents of this concept argue that developing emotional intelligence is crucial for personal growth, effective communication and building strong relationships.

When we explore the works of researchers like Daniel Goleman and Peter Salovey, we find that the concept of Emotional Intelligence (EI) has been identified as an alternative framework for understanding intelligence and therefore a vital aspect of human intelligence. Further delving into the significance of emotional intelligence in various areas of life, including personal relationships, professional success, and overall well-being reveals how emotional intelligence can enhance our ability to connect with others, effectively communicate, manage conflicts and build strong, meaningful relationships. And this is where the need to embracing emotions as valuable information comes in.

For centuries we have challenged the perception of emotions being irrational or disruptive, neglecting their importance as sources of valuable information. However, the truth is that by incorporating emotions into our decision-making process, we can gain deeper insights and make choices aligned with our values and well-being, thus the need to reframe our relationship with emotions and view them as allies rather than obstacles

1.3 Thinking with Your Heart

Have you ever realized that the heart does not just pump blood, but also helps you in understanding how others feel and how to be good to others? And why is that important?

Because being smart and intelligent is no longer about using our brain to solve problems and learn new things alone, the horizons are expanded into being caring, kind and understanding. When we use our hearts to think, we can learn to be good listeners, help others and make others feel happy. It is like having two special ways of being smart – one in our heads and one in our hearts. And when we use both, we can do amazing things and make the world a better place for everyone!

And isn't that a step forward to becoming a better version of yourself?

Therefore, thinking through the heart offers a compelling invitation to reevaluate intelligence in a way that celebrates the profound synergy between cognitive abilities and emotional intelligence. By embracing the heart as a vital center of intelligence, we can embark on a journey towards a more inclusive, empathetic and enlightened understanding of what it means to be truly intelligent.

I was trying to explain this concept to my teenage child through a fictitious woven story and this is what it was...

Story Title: The Empath's Dilemma

In a world where technological advancements have elevated the supremacy of rationality and logic, a mysterious phenomenon begins to unfold. Individuals across the globe start

experiencing a profound awakening of their empathic abilities, triggering a series of extraordinary events that challenge the conventional understanding of intelligence and wisdom.

The story follows the journey of Maya, a young woman living in a society where the pursuit of knowledge is centered around the analytical capacities of the mind. However, Maya was born with a unique gift – an exceptionally heightened sense of empathy that allows her to perceive and understand the emotions and thoughts of those around her in a deeply profound manner.

As Maya's empathic abilities continue to strengthen, she becomes increasingly aware of a subtle but powerful undercurrent of interconnectedness that binds all living beings. She begins to sense that the heart holds a reservoir of wisdom, intuition and understanding that transcends the limitations of traditional intelligence.

Amidst this awakening, a series of enigmatic occurrences unfolds worldwide. People from diverse backgrounds and cultures report experiencing inexplicable surges of empathy and compassion, leading to spontaneous acts of kindness, understanding and connection. These encounters challenge the established order, prompting individuals to question the nature of intelligence and the true source of wisdom.

As Maya delves deeper into her own empathic journey, she discovers a clandestine community of individuals who share similar experiences. Together, they uncover ancient teachings and forgotten knowledge that uphold the belief that the heart is, in fact, the new seat of intelligence and understanding.

However, their revelations draw the attention of a powerful conglomerate that seeks to maintain the status quo and suppress the burgeoning influence of empathy. As Maya and her newfound allies strive to navigate this complex and rapidly changing world, they must confront the forces that seek to stifle the emergence of the heart's wisdom and safeguard the future of humanity's newfound empathic enlightenment.

"The Empath's Dilemma" weaves a tale of discovery, empathy and resilience, as Maya and her allies embark on a daring quest to challenge the established order, embrace the wisdom of the heart and inspire a global shift toward a more empathic and interconnected world.

This story explores the transformative power of empathy and compassion and it invites readers to contemplate the profound implications of embracing the heart as the new source of intelligence and wisdom in a world that has long revered the supremacy of the mind.

In *Shakespearean language*, we can express the idea of emotional intelligence metaphorically using the linguistic style of the renowned playwright.

Here is an attempt to capture the concept in Shakespearean language:

Title: The Heart's Resurgence: A New Intellect Emerges

Prologue:

In fair Verona, where minds of doth plot,

A notion grows, a truth, so bright and hot,

That heart is the new brain, they tell,

Wherein true wisdom and knowledge dwell.

Act I:

Enter, ye seekers of knowledge and thought,
Forsooth, an idea grand, by heart be wrought,
Where passion and empathy take command,
Supplanting logic, by a new brain's stand.

Act II:

Fair emotions, in hearts' chambers deep,
Guide our choices, as dreams in slumber's keep,
Within the heart, reason finds it is place,
Intuition's whispers, a guiding grace.

Act III:

O thou who doubts this heart's ascendancy,
Mark well it is power, in love's sweet currency,
For through the heart's lens, truth doth shine,
Revealing paths that reason can't define.

4Act IV:

Let empathy pervade, thy heart open,
In understanding, bridges shall be woven,
As thy heart feels, a new wisdom springs,
A union of intellect, wherein it sings.

Act V:

Thus, in the realm where Shakespeare's words doth chime,
We find a truth befitting our present time,
The heart, wherein a new brain takes it is throne,
Guiding our souls, as we journey alone.

Epilogue:

Henceforth, let hearts prevail, in wisdom's quest,

For in passion and love, we truly invest,

Embrace this truth, dear friends, and proclaim,

Heart is the new brain, in Shakespeare's name.

Conclusion:

This chapter aims at expanding the definition of intelligence and embracing the concept of emotional intelligence. By recognizing the limitations of a purely logical approach and acknowledging the value of emotions and intuition, we open ourselves up to a more holistic understanding of intelligence. This expanded perspective sets the stage for further exploration of the heart's role in decision-making, relationship and personal growth in the subsequent chapters.

CHAPTER 2:

THE LANGUAGE OF THE HEART

The heart, often thought of as the symbol of love, holds its own special language that doesn't use words. Instead, it communicates through feelings, emotions and connections with others. The heart's language is like a secret code that everyone can understand, no matter where they're from or what language they speak. It's a way to share love and kindness without needing to say a single word. When we use the heart's language, we can make others feel special, cared for and understood.

When we talk about the "heart's language" we are talking about the ways our emotions and caring instincts help us understand and connect with the people and world around us. Just like when you feel happy, excited, or sad, your heart is speaking its own language. It is the warm feeling you get when you are with your family, the tingly excitement when you see your best friend, or the little tug in your chest when you see someone who needs help. These are all ways your heart communicates without saying a word.

The heart's language is also about understanding how others feel. When you notice that someone is sad and you give them a hug or a kind word, you're speaking the heart's language. It's like a secret code that helps us show love, kindness and compassion to the people we care about. But the heart's language isn't just about people – it's also about nature, animals and the world around us. When you feel a special connection with a pet, or when you admire a beautiful sunset, that's your heart's language telling you how much you care.

So, the heart's language is all about feelings, connections and understanding. It's about being kind, caring and showing love in the little things we do every day. By listening to the language of the heart, we can spread happiness, make others feel loved and create a world filled with warmth and compassion. Sometimes, when we're sad or worried, it can be hard to talk about our feelings. That's when the heart's language becomes really important. A comforting hug, a friendly smile, or a kind gesture can speak volumes and make someone feel better, even when we don't know what to say.

The heart's language also helps us build friendships and make new friends. When we share our toys, listen to others, and help someone who's feeling down, we're using the heart's language to show that we care. And when we feel cared for in return, it's like a special conversation that makes our hearts feel happy and warm. Even when we grow up, the heart's language stays with us. It helps us be good friends, supportive family members and kind members of our community. It's a way to spread happiness and bring people together, no matter how old we are.

A fiction story might help clear the idea better...

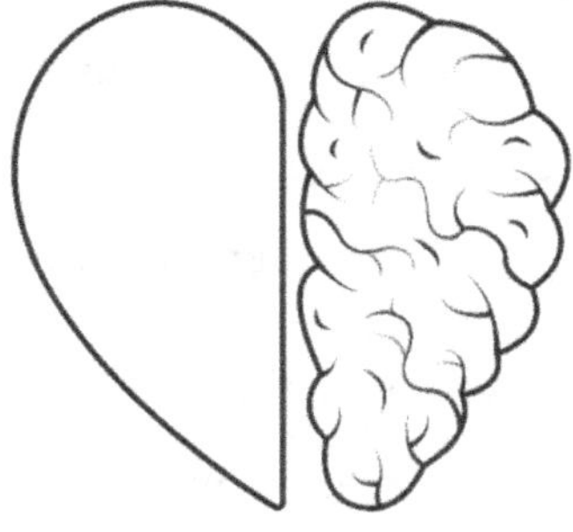

Story Title: The Heart's Wisdom

In the age of great transformation, a revelation swept across the world, challenging the very foundations of knowledge and understanding. It began in the city of Lumina, a place where the pursuit of wisdom and intellect was held in the highest esteem. This was a society where logic, reason and analytical thinking were revered above all else and the mind was exalted as the supreme arbiter of truth.

In Lumina, the Council of Cognition, a venerable assembly of scholars and intellectuals, held sway over matters of governance and decision-making. Their meticulous analyses and rational deliberations guided the city's progress, shaping policies and charting the course of it is future.

Yet, amidst this celebration of the intellect, there existed a young woman named Aria, whose perspective on life diverged from the prevailing wisdom of her time. Aria possessed a rare sensitivity to the emotions and inner turmoil of those around her. She could discern the unspoken truths that lay hidden within the hearts of others and her empathy knew no bounds.

From a young age, Aria had felt the stirrings of something profound within her own heart, a wellspring of understanding and compassion that defied the rational explanations of the mind. Her unconventional insights often led her to question the prevailing notions of wisdom and knowledge and she yearned to explore the depths of her own heart's wisdom.

One fateful day, a crisis of unprecedented magnitude struck Lumina. A bitter conflict erupted between two rival factions, each vying for dominance and refusing to yield to the other.

The city was plunged into turmoil and the Council of Cognition found it itself at an impasse, unable to reconcile the opposing factions through the usual channels of reason and logic.

Amidst the escalating discord, Aria felt a profound yearning within her heart, urging her to seek a path toward understanding and reconciliation. Listening to the whispers of her own heart, she embarked on a journey that would forever alter the course of her life and the destiny of her world.

Venturing beyond the confines of the city, Aria traversed untamed landscapes and crossed treacherous terrain, guided by an unyielding faith in the wisdom of her heart. Her quest led her to the secluded sanctuary of the Sage of Serenity, a legendary figure renowned for her profound connection to the mysteries of the heart.

The Sage, a venerable woman with eyes that seemed to hold the wisdom of ages, welcomed Aria with a gentle smile. Sensing the turmoil that weighed heavily upon Aria's heart, the Sage guided her through a series of contemplative exercises and meditative practices, encouraging her to delve into the depths of her own heart's wisdom.

As days turned into weeks, Aria experienced a profound awakening within herself, uncovering the interconnectedness of all hearts and the boundless potential for empathy and understanding that lay dormant within each individual. She came to understand that the heart, with it is capacity for compassion and intuition, held a wisdom that transcended the limitations of the mind.

Armed with this newfound insight, Aria returned to Lumina, determined to share the wisdom of the heart with her fellow citizens. She spoke of the transformative power of empathy and compassion, urging them to listen to the whispers of their own hearts and to seek understanding beyond the confines of reason

Aria's impassioned words resonated with many, stirring a quiet revolution within the hearts of the people. Slowly but steadily, a transformation began to take root as individuals from all walks of life embraced the wisdom of the heart, setting aside their preconceptions and reaching out to one another with empathy and understanding.

As the ripples of change spread throughout the city, the Council of Cognition, initially skeptical of this unconventional approach, began to take notice. They observed the burgeoning connections and heartfelt dialogues that were knitting the fractured fabric of Lumina's society back together and they could not deny the palpable impact of the heart's wisdom.

Intrigued and perhaps a bit apprehensive, the Council extended an invitation to Aria, eager to hear her perspective on navigating the city's crisis. Aria, with unwavering confidence in the transformative power of the heart, accepted the summons, ready to share her vision of empathy-led reconciliation.

Standing before the esteemed members of the Council, Aria spoke from the depths of her heart, weaving a narrative that resonated with the unspoken yearnings of those present. She implored them to consider the profound wisdom that lay within each individual's heart and to recognize the potential for empathy and understanding as the cornerstone of true wisdom.

Her words, infused with the sincerity and conviction of her own heart, sparked a spirited dialogue among the council members. Though initially met with skepticism and resistance, Aria's impassioned plea gradually found resonance within the hearts of the councilors, prompting them to embark on a journey of introspection and reevaluation.

In the weeks that followed, the Council of Cognition, inspired by Aria's vision and guided by the stirring of their own hearts, initiated a series of transformative measures. They fostered open forums for dialogue, encouraging citizens from all factions to come together and share their stories, fears and hopes. They sought to understand the root causes of the conflict, not solely through the lens of reason, but with an empathetic embrace of the diverse perspectives that had fueled the strife.

As the lines of communication opened and hearts began to unfurl, a profound shift took hold within the city. Through heartfelt conversations and acts of kindness, Lumina's citizens embraced the wisdom of the heart, forging connections that transcended the boundaries of division and mistrust.

In the wake of this transformative movement, the once-warring factions found common ground, discovering shared aspirations and a newfound appreciation for one another's unique perspectives. The seeds of empathy and understanding, sown by the wisdom of the heart, blossomed into a vibrant tapestry of unity and reconciliation.

As Lumina emerged from the crucible of conflict, the city's transformation became a beacon of hope for the world at large.

Aria's unwavering belief in the heart's wisdom had ignited a revolution, challenged the prevailing notions of knowledge and understood. The city's journey from discord to harmony stood as a testament to the transformative power of empathy and compassion and it reverberated across the lands, inspiring others to seek wisdom beyond the confines of the mind.

In the years that followed, the Council of Cognition underwent a profound metamorphosis, integrating the principles of empathy and understanding into the very fabric of their decision-making process. The heart's wisdom, once a radical notion, had become an integral part of Lumina's governance, guiding the city toward a future where the collective wisdom and compassion of it is citizens formed the bedrock of progress and unity.

Throughout the world, the story of Lumina's transformation spread like wildfire, sparking conversations and debates about the nature of wisdom and the role of empathy in governance and decision-making. In distant lands, communities and leaders took note, reevaluating their own approaches to conflict resolution and societal harmony.

The ripple effects of Aria's journey and the resurgence of the heart's wisdom transcended the boundaries of nations and cultures, inspiring a global movement toward empathetic governance and compassionate leadership. The once-radical idea that the heart could serve as the new brain, guiding humanity toward a more harmonious and understanding existence, gained a foothold in the collective consciousness of the world.

In the years that followed, Lumina continued to flourish as a shining example of the transformative power of the heart's wisdom. The city's streets resounded with the laughter of children from all backgrounds and it is citizens, once divided by strife, stood united in their shared journey toward a brighter future.

Aria, having played a pivotal role in Lumina's metamorphosis, continued her work as an advocate for empathy and understanding, traveling far and wide to share her experiences and insights with communities across the globe. Her unwavering commitment to the wisdom of the heart and her profound belief in the potential of humanity to transcend it is differences through compassion and understanding made her a revered figure and her words echoed in the hearts of countless individuals.

As the years turned into decades, the legacy of Lumina's transformation endured, shaping the course of history and inspiring generations to come. The heart's wisdom, once dismissed as a fanciful notion, had become an indelible part of the human experience, guiding societies toward a more empathetic, inclusive and harmonious future.

And so, in a world where the heart had become the new brain, where empathy and understanding reigned supreme, humanity charted a new course, embracing the profound wisdom that resided within the depths of every beating heart.

Conclusion:

Remember, everyone can understand the heart's language, and the more we use it, the more love, joy and understanding we can bring to the world. Whether it's with a big bear hug, a cheerful smile, or a thoughtful act of kindness, we can all speak the heart's language and make the world a brighter, happier place for everyone. Thus, through the language of the heart, we gain deeper insights into ourselves and others, thereby setting the stage for further exploration of intuition and the heart-brain connection in the subsequent chapters.

CHAPTER 3:

HARNESSING THE POWER OF THE HEART

Listening to the Heart: The Power of Intuition

What is Intuition?

Some say, *"We sometimes experience intuitive flashes, hunches and subtle nudges"* whilst others say, *"it is being magical or purely irrational, it highlights it is connection to our subconscious mind"*

But in reality, although intuitive cues often manifest through bodily sensations, emotions, or a sense of resonance or discomfort in certain situations, cultivating and trusting our intuitive abilities requires trusting our intuition and overcoming self-doubt or societal skepticism. intuition, often referred to as a "gut feeling" or inner knowing, can guide us in making wise decisions and navigating life's complexities The power of intuition underscores the idea that while rational thought and analysis are valuable, there exists a deeper, innate knowing within each individual that can offer valuable insights and guidance.

Intuition is often associated with the "heart" as opposed to the "mind", is a powerful and often overlooked tool for making choices, solving problems, and understanding the world. When we listen to our hearts, we are attuned to our emotions, instincts and subtle perceptions, which can provide valuable information that logic alone may not uncover. Acknowledging the power of intuition involves cultivating self-awareness, mindfulness, and the ability to tune into one's feelings and instincts.

Intuition often requires quieting the mind, being receptive to subtle cues, and learning to trust oneself. While intuition alone should not replace careful analysis and due diligence, intuition can provide a holistic perspective and serve as an early warning system for potential pitfalls or opportunities, absolutely valuable in decision-making and risk assessment.

In various fields such as business, leadership, creativity and personal development, many successful individuals attribute their breakthroughs to intuitive insights and following their hearts. By tapping into their intuition, individuals can access newer perspectives, unconventional ideas and novel solutions to complex problems. However, it's essential to exercise discernment when relying on intuition, as it is not infallible and can be influenced by biases, fears and other internal factors. Balancing intuition with critical thinking and external input is crucial for making well-rounded decisions.

The Power of the Heart: Emotional Intelligence

The practicality of cultivating emotional intelligence by integrating mindfulness, stress management techniques, empathy-building exercises, non-judgmental acceptance, self-compassion and intuition-strengthening practices into our daily lives, eventually leads to an experience of profound personal growth. These practices enable us to navigate emotions, manage stress, build fulfilling relationships and make wise, heart-centered decisions. By integrating intuitive decision-making with logical analysis, one can always harness the heart's intuitive intelligence to make choices aligned with one's deepest values and purpose.

When exploring the power of the heart, historical examples can provide compelling evidence of the role of emotions, intuition and empathy in decision-making and human achievement. While the phrase "the heart is the new brain" is a contemporary concept, historical figures and events can be interpreted through this lens therefore bringing forth the deep-rooted practices since centuries for cultivating emotional intelligence.

Here are a few *historical examples* that could be considered in the context of this concept:

1. **Abraham Lincoln's Leadership:** Abraham Lincoln, the 16th President of the United States, is often celebrated for his exceptional leadership during the American Civil War. His ability to empathize with others, understand their perspectives, and show compassion is indicative of emotional intelligence. His leadership style and decision-making process could be analyzed to illustrate the role of the heart in effective leadership.

2. **Mahatma Gandhi's Nonviolent Resistance:** Mahatma Gandhi, the leader of the Indian independence movement, is known for his philosophy of nonviolent resistance. His approach was deeply rooted in empathy, compassion and understanding. Gandhi's ability to inspire and lead through emotional intelligence and moral authority is an example of the heart's influence on social change.

3. **Florence Nightingale's Nursing Reforms:** Florence Nightingale, a pioneer of modern nursing, is remembered for her compassionate care and advocacy for sanitary conditions in hospitals. Her work was driven by a deep sense of empathy and intuition, leading to significant reforms in healthcare practices.

4. **Martin Luther King Jr.'s Civil Rights Movement:** Martin Luther King Jr., a prominent leader in the American civil rights movement, demonstrated exceptional emotional intelligence in his efforts to advocate for justice and equality. His ability to connect with people on an emotional level and inspire change through empathy and understanding is a powerful example of the heart's influence in social and political movements.

These historical examples, among many others, provide insight into how individuals have utilized emotional intelligence, intuition and empathy to effect positive change and make significant contributions to society. By examining these figures through the lens of "the heart is the new brain", one can illustrate how these qualities have played a crucial role in shaping the course of history and influencing the world.

Conclusion:

This chapter aims at highlighting the power of intuition and its connection to the heart. It focuses on historical instances and practical strategies for harnessing the power of the heart. By tapping into the wellspring of heart's wisdom one can be guided towards greater personal growth, authentic decision-making and a sense of purpose. This chapter lays the groundwork for further exploration of the power of the heart in professional settings and relationships in the upcoming chapters as well as sets the stage for further exploration of the heart's profound influence and its intricate connection with the brain in the subsequent chapters.

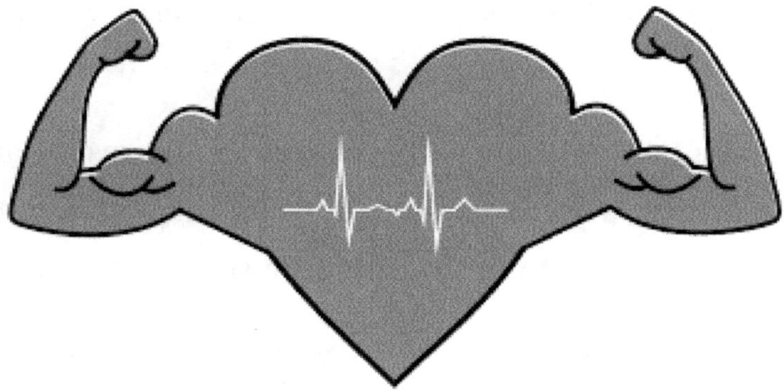

CHAPTER 4:

BRIDGING THE GAP: THE HEART - BRAIN CONNECTION

In this chapter, we explore the fascinating and intricate connection between the heart and the brain. We delve into the scientific understanding of this connection and how it impacts our emotions, thoughts and overall well-being. By understanding the heart-brain connection, we gain insights into how our physiological and emotional states influence each other and can harness this knowledge for personal growth and a balanced life.

4.1 Understanding the science behind the heart-brain interaction

The heart-brain interaction is a complex and fascinating area of study that involves the intricate relationship between the cardiovascular system and the central nervous system.

Here are some key aspects of the science behind heart-brain interaction:

a. **Neurocardiology:** Neurocardiology is the field of study that explores the interactions between the heart and the brain at a physiological and biochemical level. It focuses on understanding how the brain and the heart communicate with each other through neural and hormonal pathways. Research in neurocardiology has revealed that the heart has its intrinsic nervous system, often referred to as the "heart brain," which can function independently of the brain in the head.

b. **Autonomic Nervous System:** The autonomic nervous system ('ANS') plays a central role in mediating the communication between the heart and the brain. The ANS consists of two main branches: the sympathetic nervous system ('SNS') and the parasympathetic nervous system ('PNS'). The SNS is involved in the "fight or flight" response, promoting increased heart rate and cardiac output, while the PNS helps regulate resting heart rate and promotes relaxation.

c. **Heart Rate Variability ('HRV'):** HRV refers to the variation in the time interval between heartbeats. It is an important indicator of the interplay between the sympathetic and parasympathetic branches of the ANS. Higher HRV is generally associated with better overall health and reflects the adaptability and resilience of the cardiovascular and nervous systems.

d. **Emotions and the Heart:** Research has shown that emotions can influence heart function and vice versa. For example, experiencing stress or anxiety can lead to increased sympathetic activity and higher heart rate, while positive emotions and relaxation can promote parasympathetic dominance and lower heart rate.

e. **Hormonal Communication:** The heart and the brain also communicate through the release of hormones and neurotransmitters. For instance, the heart produces and releases hormones such as atrial natriuretic peptide ('ANP') and brain natriuretic peptide ('BNP'), which play a role in regulating blood pressure and fluid balance.

f. **Clinical Implications:** Understanding the heart-brain interaction has important clinical implications. For example, it has led to the development of interventions such as biofeedback and mindfulness-based therapies that aim to improve heart health by modulating the activity of the central and autonomic nervous systems.

g. **The Vagus Nerve:** The Vagus nerve is a key component of the parasympathetic nervous system and plays a crucial role in mediating the bi-directional communication between the heart and the brain. It carries signals from the brain to the heart and other internal organs, influencing functions such as heart rate, digestion and inflammation. Stimulation of the Vagus nerve has been explored as a potential therapeutic approach for conditions such as heart disease, depression and epilepsy.

h. **Cognitive Function and Cardiovascular Health:** Research has shown that cardiovascular health can significantly impact cognitive function and vice versa. Poor cardiovascular health, including conditions such as hypertension and atherosclerosis, has been linked to an increased risk of cognitive decline and dementia. Conversely, maintaining good cardiovascular health through exercise, a healthy diet and stress management can support brain health and cognitive function.

i. **Heart-Brain Axis:** The concept of the "heart-brain axis" emphasizes the bi-directional communication and influence between the heart and the brain. This axis involves not only neural and hormonal pathways but also immune signaling and the effects of inflammation. Dysregulation of the heart-brain axis has been implicated in various conditions, including heart failure, arrhythmias, anxiety disorders and depression.

j. **Psychophysiological Coherence:** Psychophysiolo - gical coherence refers to a state of optimal functioning in which the heart, brain and other bodily systems are in sync and working harmoniously. This state is characterized by smooth, balanced heart rhythm patterns and is associated with improved cognitive performance, emotional stability and overall well-being. Practices such as HRV biofeedback and heart-focused breathing aim to promote psychophysiological coherence.

k. **Stress and Resilience:** Chronic stress can have detrimental effects on both the heart and the brain, contributing to the development of cardiovascular disease, hypertension and mental health disorders. Understanding the mechanisms through which stress impacts the heart-brain interaction has led to the development of stress management techniques and resilience-building strategies aimed at mitigating these effects.

l. **Holistic Approaches to Health:** The study of heart-brain interaction has contributed to a broader understanding of the interconnectedness of physical, mental and emotional health. This has led to the promotion of holistic approaches to health care that recognize the influence of psychological and emotional factors on cardiovascular health and the importance of addressing both physical and mental well-being.

Overall, the science behind heart-brain interaction is a multidisciplinary field that encompasses neurobiology, cardiology, psychology and more. Ongoing research in this area continues to uncover new insights into the intricate connections between the heart and the brain and their impact on overall health and well-being.

4.2 The heart's electromagnetic field and the impact on brain

The heart's electromagnetic field has been found to have an impact on brain function and overall cognitive processes. Research in the field of neurocardiology, which explores the interactions between the heart and the brain, has revealed several ways in which the heart's electromagnetic field influences the brain:

a. **Coherence between Heart and Brain:** When the heart is in a coherent state, characterized by a harmonious and balanced rhythm, it has been shown to have a positive impact on brain function. Studies have found that coherent heart rhythms are associated with increased synchronization and coherence in brainwave patterns, particularly in the prefrontal cortex, an area of the brain associated with higher cognitive functions.

b. **Emotional Regulation:** The heart's electromagnetic field can influence emotional processing and regulation in the brain. Coherent heart rhythms have been linked to improved emotional regulation, leading to greater emotional stability, reduced anxiety and enhanced resilience to stress. This can result in more balanced and coherent brain activity related to emotional processing.

c. **Cognitive Performance:** Research has suggested that heart coherence can enhance cognitive performance. When the heart's electromagnetic field is coherent, it has been associated with improved mental clarity, focus and cognitive function. This may be due to the influence of the heart's rhythms on the brain's information processing and executive functions.

d. **Interoception:** The heart's electromagnetic field plays a role in interoception, the ability to sense and interpret the body's internal signals. This includes the communication of information from the heart to the brain, influencing processes related to self-awareness, emotional experience and decision-making.

e. **Social Interactions:** The electromagnetic field of the heart has implications for social interactions and communication. Coherent heart rhythms have been associated with improved social cognition, empathy and the ability to connect with others, suggesting that the heart's field may play a role in interpersonal relationships and social behavior.

Overall, the heart's electromagnetic field and its impact on brain function represent a fascinating area of research that is shedding light on the intricate connections between the cardiovascular system and the brain. Understanding these interactions may have implications for fields such as psychology, neuroscience and the development of interventions aimed at improving mental and emotional well-being.

4.3 The impact of emotions on the heart and the brain

Emotions can have a significant impact on both the heart and the brain. Here's a brief overview of how emotions affect these two vital organs:

Impact on the Heart:

a. **Stress and negative emotions:** Chronic stress and negative emotions like anger, anxiety and depression can have a direct impact on the heart. They can lead to increased blood pressure, elevated heart rate and the release of stress hormones like cortisol and adrenaline, which can contribute to the development of cardiovascular diseases such as hypertension, heart disease and stroke.

b. **Positive emotions and heart health:** On the other hand, positive emotions like happiness, love and gratitude can have a beneficial impact on the heart. They are associated with lower levels of stress hormones and can lead to improved cardiovascular health and a reduced risk of heart disease.

Impact on the Brain:

a. **Emotional processing:** Emotions are processed in various regions of the brain, including the amygdala, prefrontal cortex and insula. These areas are involved in interpreting and responding to emotional stimuli and they play a crucial role in regulating emotional responses and behaviors.

b. **Memory and learning:** Emotions can significantly impact memory and learning. Emotional events are often better remembered than neutral ones, and the amygdala plays a key role in this process. Emotional arousal can enhance memory formation and emotional experiences can shape cognitive processes.

c. **Neurotransmitters and mood regulation:** Emotions are closely tied to the release of neurotransmitters in the brain, such as serotonin, dopamine and norepinephrine, which play key roles in regulating mood, motivation and pleasure. Imbalances in these neurotransmitters are associated with mood disorders like depression and anxiety.

Overall, the impact of emotions on the heart and brain is complex and multifaceted. Both positive and negative emotions can exert profound effects on these organs, influencing everything from cardiovascular health to cognitive processes and emotional well-being.

4.4 Applying heart-brain coherence in daily life for increased creativity, resilience and well-being

a. **Sleep and Stress Management:** Adequate sleep and effective stress management are crucial for nurturing a strong heart-brain connection. Chronic stress can have detrimental effects on both the heart and brain, while quality sleep is essential for cognitive function and emotional regulation. Prioritizing good sleep hygiene and implementing stress-reduction techniques such as yoga, progressive muscle relaxation, or engaging in hobbies can contribute to a healthier heart-brain relationship.

b. **Creative Expression and Artistic Pursuits:** Engaging in creative activities, such as art, music, or writing, can be therapeutic and beneficial for the heart-brain connection. Creative expression has been shown to positively impact emotions, reduce stress and enhance cognitive function. By tapping into creative outlets, individuals can foster a deeper connection between their emotional experiences and cognitive processes, contributing to a more integrated heart-brain relationship.

c. **Cognitive Training and Mental Stimulation:** Keeping the brain engaged and active through cognitive training and mental stimulation can contribute to overall brain health. Activities such as puzzles, learning new skills, or engaging in intellectually stimulating conversations can help maintain cognitive function and support the interconnectedness of the heart and brain.

d. **Holistic Health Practices:** Exploring holistic health practices such as acupuncture, traditional Chinese medicine, or Ayurveda can provide additional avenues for promoting balance and harmony within the body. These practices often consider the interplay between the heart and brain as part of a larger interconnected system, offering complementary approaches to supporting overall well-being.

e. **Professional Support:** Seeking guidance from healthcare professionals, such as psychologists, counselors, or integrative medicine practitioners, can provide tailored support for individuals looking to bridge the gap in their heart-brain connection. These professionals can offer personalized strategies, therapeutic interventions and lifestyle recommendations to address specific emotional and cognitive needs, ultimately contributing to a more balanced heart-brain relationship.

Conclusion:

This chapter emphasizes the profound impact of the heart-brain connection on our emotions, thoughts and well-being by delving on the scientific connections between the two. By understanding and nurturing this connection, we can enhance our emotional intelligence, self-regulation and overall balance. By embracing practices that promote coherence, we can harness the power of the heart-brain connection for personal growth, improved relationships and a greater sense of well-being.

CHAPTER 5:

THE HEART AT WORK IN PROFESSIONAL SETTINGS

We are all aware that in recent times, the qualities of compassion, understanding and emotional awareness, in professional settings, have increasingly become valuable in the modern workplace in addition to the traditional cognitive and analytical skills

In professional settings, the concept of *the heart as the new brain* can be supported in several ways:

a. Emphasizing Emotional Intelligence: Encouraging individuals in organizations to develop their emotional intelligence can lead to better communication, stronger relationships and more effective leadership. This can be achieved through training programs, workshops and coaching that focus on self-awareness, self-regulation, empathy and social skills.

b. Promoting a Positive Work Environment: Cultivating a workplace culture that values kindness, respect and empathy can contribute to employee well-being and motivation. Leaders can support this by leading with compassion, recognizing and celebrating achievements and fostering a sense of belonging within the organization.

c. Encouraging Authentic Leadership: Authentic leaders are genuine, transparent and guided by strong moral principles. By promoting authentic leadership, organizations can create an environment where individuals feel valued, understood and empowered to bring their whole selves to work.

d. Prioritizing Employee Well-being: Recognizing the importance of work-life balance, mental health and overall well-being can contribute to a more engaged and productive workforce. Providing resources for stress management, offering flexible work arrangements and promoting a healthy work environment are ways to support this priority.

e. Building Meaningful Relationships: Encouraging teamwork, collaboration and open communication can foster a sense of community within the organization. When individuals feel connected and supported by their colleagues, they are more likely to contribute their best efforts and feel a sense of fulfillment in their work.

f. Empowering Servant Leadership: Servant leadership emphasizes the leader's role as a servant to others, prioritizing the needs of their team members and empowering them to reach their full potential. By promoting servant leadership, organizations can create a culture of support, trust and empowerment.\

g. Encouraging Compassionate Communication: Effective communication is essential in any professional setting and integrating compassionate communication techniques can lead to better understanding, conflict resolution and overall team cohesion. Conflicts are a common occurrence in the workplace and emotional intelligence plays a vital role in resolving them constructively. This may involve active listening, expressing empathy and promoting open, honest dialogue fostering respect.

h. Recognizing and Rewarding Empathy: Acknowledging and rewarding acts of empathy and kindness in the workplace can reinforce the value of emotional intelligence and compassionate behavior. This can be done through recognition programs, performance evaluations, or other forms of acknowledgment.

i. Integrating Mindfulness Practices: Mindfulness practices, such as meditation programs and deep breathing exercises or other mindfulness activities can help employees manage stress, improve focus and enhance their emotional well-being.

j. Embracing Diversity and Inclusion: Fostering a diverse and inclusive workplace promotes empathy, understanding and a broader perspective among employees. Encouraging diverse perspectives, embracing differences and creating a sense of belonging for all individuals can contribute to a more empathetic and emotionally intelligent work environment.

k. Supporting Personal Growth and Development: Providing opportunities for personal and professional development, such as mentorship programs, skill-building workshops and continued education, can demonstrate an investment in the well-being and growth of employees, fostering a culture of care and support.

1. Measuring Success Beyond Financial Metrics: Evaluating success in the workplace should not be limited to financial performance alone. Organizations can assess their impact on employees' well-being, satisfaction and sense of purpose as key indicators of success.

By embracing these approaches, organizations can create a workplace environment that values emotional intelligence, empathy, and human connection, ultimately contributing to the well-being and success of their employees. This, in turn, can lead to greater innovation, collaboration and overall organizational performance.

Here are two hypothetical scenarios at work that exemplify the concept of "Heart is the New Brain" and highlight the significance of emotional intelligence in decision-making and overall development in a professional set up.

Case Study 1:

Sarah – Embracing Emotional Intelligence for a Critical Decision Making at Work

Meet Sarah, a marketing executive at a fast-growing tech startup. She's faced with a critical decision; the company is considering a major rebranding initiative that could potentially alienate the existing customer base while attracting a new demographic. The data and market research overwhelmingly support the rebrand, pointing to potential growth and increased market share. However, Sarah feels a deep sense of unease about the proposed changes, despite the logical arguments in favor of the rebrand.

In this scenario, Sarah's head (representing rational thought and analysis) is in conflict with her heart (representing intuition and emotional intelligence). She decides to listen to her intuition and advocates for a more gradual and inclusive rebranding strategy that takes into account the concerns of the current customer base while still appealing to the new target audience.

As a result, the company's leadership team initially hesitates, but they ultimately follow Sarah's recommendation. The rebranding process becomes a collaborative effort involving the existing customers, incorporating their feedback and addressing their concerns. The result is a successful rebrand that not only attracts new customers but also strengthens the loyalty of the existing customer base, leading to increased customer satisfaction and long-term growth.

This hypothetical scenario demonstrates the application of "the heart is the new brain" concept in a business context. By listening to her intuition and considering the emotional impact of the decision, Sarah was able to guide the company toward a more balanced and empathetic approach, resulting in a positive outcome for both the business and it is customers.

In this way, the scenario illustrates how emotional intelligence, intuition and empathy, often associated with the heart, can play a pivotal role in decision-making processes, even in a highly analytical and data-driven environment.

Case Study 2

Laura - Embracing Emotional Intelligence in Career Transition

Laura, a successful corporate executive, feels unfulfilled and disconnected from her work. Despite her professional achievements, she yearns for a career that aligns with her passions and values. Recognizing the importance of emotional intelligence, she decides to embark on a journey of self-discovery and personal growth.

Laura starts by tapping into her emotions and listening to her heart's desires. Through introspection and self-reflection, she identifies her true passions and core values. She explores various avenues and pursues opportunities that resonate with her heart, even if they may require stepping outside her comfort zone.

As she embraces emotional intelligence, Laura navigates the challenges and uncertainties by trusting her intuition and making authentic decisions. She seeks guidance from mentors and connects with individuals who share her aspirations. She understands the importance of building relationships based on empathy, active listening and open communication.

Through this transformative process, Laura discovers a new career path that ignites her passion and allows her to make a positive impact in the world. By relying on her emotional intelligence, she finds fulfillment and a sense of purpose, realizing that the heart's wisdom guides her towards a more fulfilling and meaningful professional life.

Conclusion:

This chapter illustrates the significance of emotional intelligence in professional settings. By incorporating the heart's wisdom into our work lives, we can enhance communication, resolve conflicts, demonstrate effective leadership and make sound decisions. Cultivating emotional intelligence creates positive work environments, improves job satisfaction and leads to greater professional success and fulfillment. This chapter also sets the stage for further exploration of emotional intelligence in personal relationships and nurturing a sense of connection in the next chapter.

CHAPTER 6:

RELATIONSHIPS AND CONNECTION: THE HEART'S IMPACT

Understanding the heart's impact in relationships and connections involves recognizing the emotional, empathetic, and intuitive aspects of human interactions. While the brain is responsible for cognitive functions and decision-making, the heart symbolizes emotions, empathy and deeper connections with others. We explore how individuals can cultivate a compassionate heart and we provide insights into the transformative power of compassion in fostering personal well-being, nurturing meaningful relationships and contributing to a more harmonious and empathetic society.

Here are several key points to consider when understanding the heart's impact in relationships and connections:

i. Emotional Awareness: The heart plays a crucial role in emotional awareness within relationships. It involves recognizing and understanding one's own emotions as well as being attuned to the feelings of others. Emotional awareness enables individuals to navigate interactions with empathy and sensitivity, fostering deeper connections and mutual understanding.

ii. Empathy and Compassion: Empathy, often associated with the heart, involves the ability to understand and share the feelings of others. Compassion, an extension of empathy, drives individuals to act with kindness and consideration toward others. These qualities are essential for building strong, supportive connections and nurturing meaningful relationships.

iii. Intuition and Gut Feelings: The heart is often linked to intuition and "gut feelings," which can guide individuals in their interactions with others. Intuition can provide valuable insights into social dynamics, helping people navigate relationships and make decisions with consideration for others' emotions. Trusting one's intuition can lead to more authentic and fulfilling connections.

iv. Vulnerability and Authenticity: The heart's impact in relationships also involves vulnerability and authenticity. Opening one's heart to others, sharing feelings and experiences and being authentic in communication can foster trust and intimacy, leading to deeper and more meaningful connections.

v. Emotional Resilience: The heart influences emotional resilience, which is essential for maintaining healthy relationships. Emotional resilience enables individuals to effectively cope with challenges, conflicts and setbacks in relationships, leading to greater stability and well-being in interpersonal connections.

vi. Physical and Emotional Well-Being: The heart's impact on relationships extends to physical and emotional well-being. Positive social connections and emotional support have been linked to improved health and overall well-being. Cultivating strong, heart-centered connections can contribute to greater happiness and fulfillment in life.

vii. Communication and Connection: Effective communication is fundamental to building and maintaining healthy relationships. Heart-centered communication involves expressing emotions, active listening and fostering open, honest dialogue. When individuals communicate from the heart, they can build deeper connections and create a sense of emotional intimacy with others.

viii. Love and Affection: The heart is often associated with love, affection, and care. Expressing love and affection in relationships nurtures a sense of connection and belonging. Whether in romantic relationships, friendships, or familial connections, the expression of love from the heart is a powerful force that strengthens bonds and fosters a sense of security and well-being.

ix. Empowerment and Support: The heart's impact in relationships also involves empowerment and support. By offering encouragement, understanding, and emotional support, individuals can uplift and empower their loved ones. This support can create a sense of safety and trust within relationships, fostering a strong sense of connection and mutual growth.

x. Forgiveness and Healing: The heart plays a crucial role in forgiveness and healing within relationships. Forgiveness is an act of compassion and understanding that can lead to emotional healing and reconciliation. By letting go of past hurts and embracing forgiveness, individuals can pave the way for deeper, more authentic connections with others.

xi. Shared Values and Emotional Alignment: Building meaningful connections often involves shared values and emotional alignment. When individuals connect on a heart level through shared beliefs, goals and emotional resonance, they can form strong, enduring connections based on mutual understanding and harmony.

xii. Emotional Bonds and Trust: Heart-centered connections are built on emotional bonds and trust. Trust is the foundation of healthy relationships, and it is nurtured through consistent, heartfelt interactions, emotional reliability and mutual respect. When trust is present, relationships can deepen and individuals can feel secure in their connections with others.

Here are two case studies that illustrate the significance of emotional intelligence and the heart's impact on relationships.

Case Study 1:

Sarah and John - Enhancing Relationship through Emotional Intelligence

Sarah and John have been in a committed relationship for several years. However, they have recently been experiencing frequent misunderstandings and conflicts. Both individuals eagerly want to improve their relationship but are struggling to effectively communicate their needs and emotions.

By embracing emotional intelligence, they decide to focus on developing their empathy and active listening skills. They engage in daily practice sessions, taking turns being the listener and speaker. During these sessions, they learn to truly listen to each other, seeking to understand and validate each other's emotions and perspectives. They practice reflective listening, paraphrasing each other's words to ensure accurate understanding.

Over time, their emotional intelligence grows, strengthening their connection and improving their communication. By embracing empathy and active listening, Sarah and John create a safe space for open and honest expression of emotions. They become more attuned to each other's needs, delivering support and validation, leading to a deeper bond and a healthier, more fulfilling relationship.

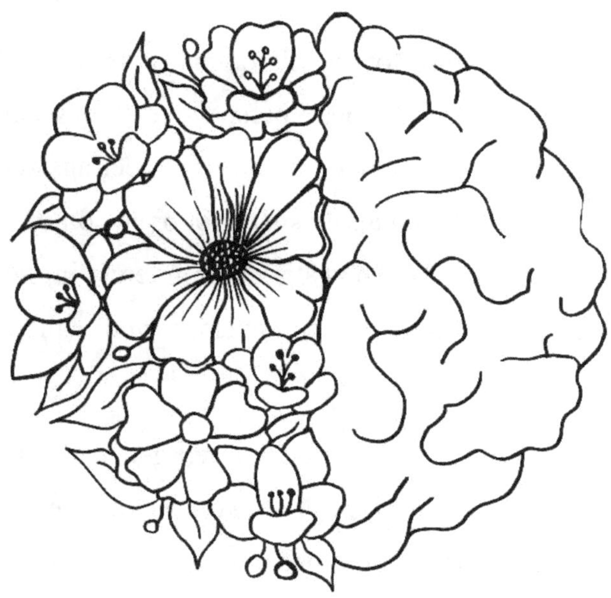

Case Study 2:

Mathew - Balancing Empathy and Boundaries in Leadership

Mathew is an ambitious leader who is known for being assertive and results-oriented. However, he has recently noticed tension and disengagement among his team members. Recognizing the importance of emotional intelligence, Matthew realizes that he needs to balance empathy with maintaining boundaries as a leader.

Mathew starts by developing his empathy skills, seeking to understand his team members' perspectives, challenges, and needs. He schedules regular one-on-one meetings with each team member, providing a safe space for open communication and active listening. He shows genuine interest in their well-being, taking the time to acknowledge and validate their emotions.

As Mathew grows his emotional intelligence, he learns to establish clear boundaries while still acknowledging and addressing his team's emotions. He sets expectations and communicates with empathy, considering each team member's emotional well-being in decision-making processes. He also encourages a supportive and collaborative work environment where team members feel seen and valued.

With this balanced approach, Mathew sees a remarkable improvement in team engagement, productivity and overall job satisfaction. By embracing empathy while maintaining appropriate boundaries, Mathew creates an environment where his team members feel heard, supported, and motivated, resulting in enhanced teamwork and success.

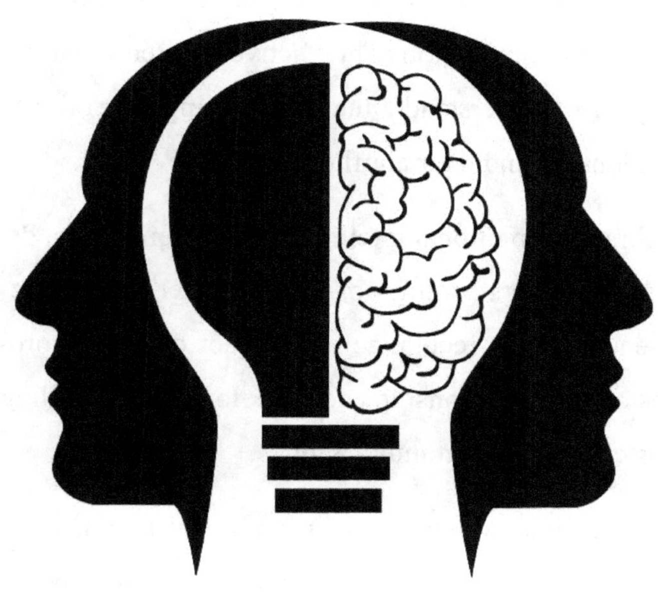

Case Study 3:

Alex - Emotional Intelligence in Relationship Repair

Alex and Maya have been in a committed relationship for several years but have been experiencing persistent conflicts and emotional distance. Recognizing the importance of emotional intelligence, they decide to work on enhancing their connection and resolving their issues.

They start by cultivating self-awareness and emotional regulation skills. Both partners take responsibility for their emotions and learn to express their needs and concerns with empathy and compassion. They actively listen to each other, seeking to understand the underlying emotions and motivations behind their conflicts.

By embracing emotional intelligence, Alex and Maya develop a deeper understanding of each other's feelings and experiences. They recognize the impact of their words and actions on their relationship and work towards rebuilding trust and fostering open communication.

As they continue to nurture their emotional intelligence, they actively practice empathy, showing understanding and support for each other's emotions. They prioritize quality time together, engaging in activities that strengthen their emotional connection and reinforce their love and commitment.

Through their dedication to emotional intelligence, Alex and Maya not only repair their relationship but also create a stronger, more resilient bond. By valuing each other's emotions and nurturing empathy, they develop a profound connection that allows them to navigate challenges more harmoniously and grow together in love and understanding.

These case studies illustrate the power of emotional intelligence and the heart's influence in decision-making, personal growth and relationship dynamics. By embracing emotional intelligence, individuals can align their actions with their authentic selves, make meaningful choices and cultivate stronger connections with others. The heart's wisdom guides us towards a more fulfilling and harmonious life.

These case studies highlight how incorporating emotional intelligence and embracing the heart's impact can lead to positive transformations in both personal and professional relationships. By developing empathy, active listening and balanced leadership, individuals can foster meaningful connections, resolve conflicts and create supportive and fulfilling environments.

Conclusion:

This chapter underlines that understanding the heart's impact in relationships and connections involves acknowledging the emotional, empathetic and intuitive dimensions of human interactions. By embracing emotional awareness, empathy, intuition, vulnerability and resilience, individuals can foster deeper and more fulfilling connections with others, ultimately contributing to a richer and more meaningful life.

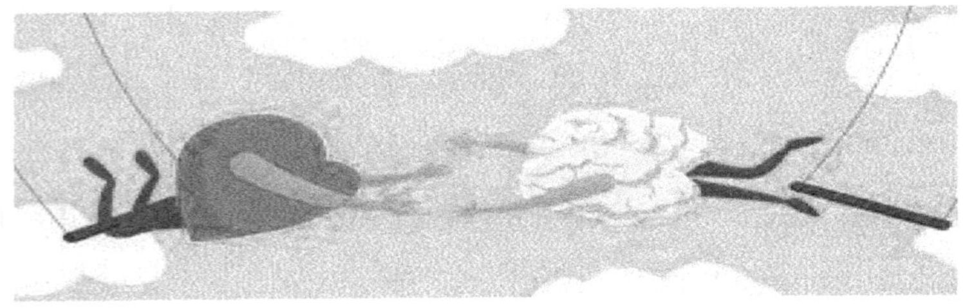

CHAPTER 7:

HOLISTIC LIVING: BALANCING HEART AND BRAIN – A ROADMAP

This chapter emphasizes the importance of embracing a holistic approach to living by balancing the wisdom of the heart and the brain to create a harmonious and fulfilling life. By cultivating this balance, we can make authentic decisions, nurture our well-being, and embrace a meaningful existence.

Afterall, *"You only live once, but if you do it right, once is enough"* -- Mae West

8.1 *Integrating emotional and intuitive guidance with logical thinking/ rational analysis* to enhance decision-making by providing valuable insights and considering the impact of choices on both ourselves and others.

8.2 *Cultivating a balanced decision-making approach that considers both the heart and the brain* for exploring and processing emotions during logical analysis and critical thinking. The benefit it provides is in way of taking time for self-reflection, introspection, seeking diverse perspectives and finding alignment between our emotions, values and logical reasoning.

8.3 *Living authentically by aligning our actions, goals and relationships with our heart's wisdom* thereby creating a life that resonates with our true selves and brings us a sense of fulfillment. Developing the ability to let go of negative emotions, past grievances and things beyond one's control can contribute to emotional balance and reduce stress and anxiety. This eventually helps in navigating life's ups and downs with greater ease and grace which is not possible by depending on the brain alone.

8.4 *Nurturing well-being through heart-centered practices* such as emotional resilience,
empathy, gratitude, compassion and self-care to create a solid foundation for living a holistic and fulfilling life. This in turn can shift focus from negative emotions to positive ones, promoting emotional balance and overall well-being. Besides, heart-focused breathing exercises, gratitude journaling, acts of kindness, mindfulness meditation and self-compassion exercises can foster a deeper connection to their own hearts and the hearts of others.

8.5 *Embracing creativity and intuition as powerful allies in our journey towards holistic living* for stimulating and nurturing creativity. For example, engaging in any creative activity such as art, music, or writing can provide an outlet for emotional expression and contribute to a sense of fulfillment and balance; it augments a growth mindset for making choices aligned with one's authentic self.

8.6 *Building connections and fostering meaningful relationships* is a key aspect in holistic living. Here, the role of empathy, active listening and open communication in nurturing relationships whilst recognizing one's limit and communicating them effectively to others to establish healthy boundaries. Fostering a supportive, non-judgmental environment for dialogue and encouraging honest and empathetic interactions in personal and professional contexts contributes to free living.

8.7 *Cultivating Heart-Centered Leadership at Work* in fostering inclusive, compassionate and purpose-driven organizations/ communities. This is achieved by empowering leaders to integrate emotional intelligence and heart-centered values into their leadership approach, driving positive change and sustainable success.

8.8 Navigating a Digital Age by not only recognizing the challenges posed by the pervasive influence of technology but rather by exploring the potential for leveraging digital tools to support instead of hindering heart-centered living. The need of the hour is navigating the digital landscape whilst maintaining a deep connection to one's heart and the hearts of others through responsible technology usage.

8.9 *Inspiring Collective Change by expanding our focus to the broader societal impact* of heart-centered living, we showcase examples of initiatives, movements and policies that prioritize empathy, compassion and social responsibility. This helps in contributing to a more heart-centered society through advocacy, community engagement and conscious consumer choices by digging in the transformative potential of collective action rooted in the wisdom of the heart. Supporting for causes that align with heart-centered values truly contributes to a more empathetic and equitable society.

Conclusion:

This chapter concludes by highlighting the transformative power of balancing the heart's wisdom and the brain's logic. This holistic approach allows us to make authentic decisions, nurture our well-being and cultivate meaningful connections. This chapter also provides practical steps for embracing the heart as the new center of intelligence thereby recognizing the opportunity to attain a profound sense of purpose in one's personal journey.

I am a foodie and couldn't have ended this topic without a metaphorical recipe for practice that symbolizes the concept of "Heart is the New Brain":

Recipe: Heart is the New Brain

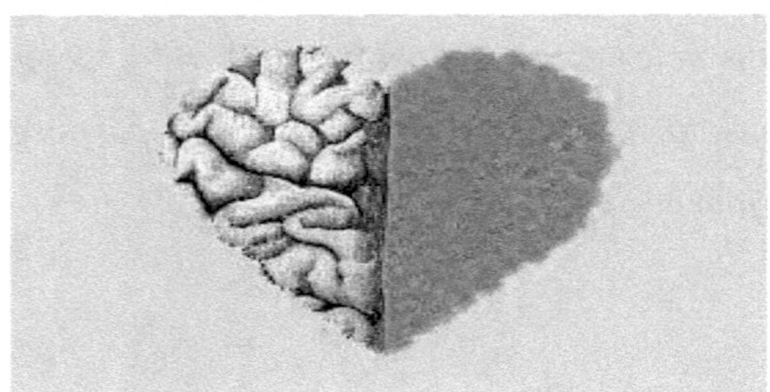

Ingredients:

Emotional intelligence, Self-awareness, Empathy, Intuition, Authenticity, Courage, Growth Mindset, Compassion

Instructions:

1. Start by cultivating emotional intelligence. Take the time to understand and recognize your own emotions and how they impact your thoughts and actions. Reflect on past experiences and gain insight into your emotional patterns and triggers.

2. Mix in a generous portion of self-awareness. Seek to understand your strengths and weaknesses, values, and aspirations. Connect with your true desires and passions, allowing your heart to guide you in making authentic choices.

3. Add empathy to the mix. Practice stepping into the shoes of others and genuinely listening to their perspectives and emotions. Embrace a compassionate mindset, seeking to understand and support those around you.

4. Listen closely to your intuition. Trust your inner voice and the messages it conveys. Take moments of silence to tune into your heart's wisdom, allowing it to guide your decisions and actions.

5. Embrace authenticity as a core ingredient. Remove the masks and pretenses, embracing your true self. Be open and vulnerable, both with yourself and others, fostering genuine connections and meaningful relationships.

6. Stir in courage and a growth mindset. Embrace challenges and setbacks as opportunities for personal growth and learning. Be willing to step out of your comfort zone and embrace new experiences, allowing your heart to lead the way.

7. Finally, sprinkle compassion throughout the mixture. Show kindness and understanding to yourself and others. Practice self-compassion, recognizing that mistakes and imperfections are part of the human experience. Extend compassion to others, creating a supportive and nurturing environment.

8. Once all the ingredients have been blended and mixed, let the mixture rest and evolve over time. Continually revisit and adjust the recipe as needed, as personal growth is an ongoing journey.

Remember, this metaphorical recipe represents the idea that by cultivating emotional intelligence, embracing authenticity, following intuition and nourishing a compassionate mindset, we can tap into the wisdom of the heart.

Allow this recipe to guide your personal transformation, embracing the concept of "Heart is the New Brain" in your life.

THE END IS THE BEGINNING

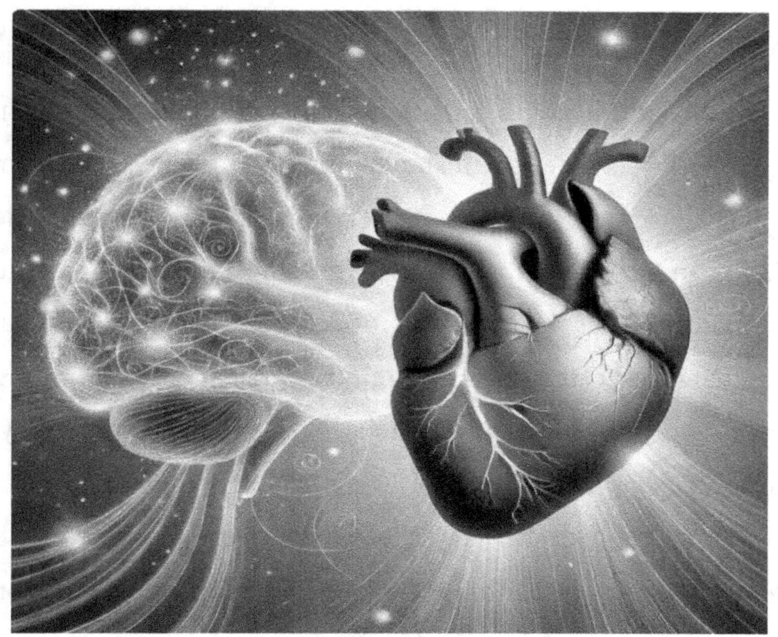

Our brain is important for logic and reasoning whilst our heart is where we feel the emotions – love, empathy, kindness, compassion, et el. Heart is the source of our intuition and it is here our true passion and desires lie.

But do we listen to our hearts more often and lead with love?

Many will say that the heart is just the muscle to pump blood so why romanticize it?

And now we know that it has its own intelligence and is capable of influencing our emotions thoughts and behavior. In our earlier chapters whilst delving into the heart – brain connection, studies suggested that the heart's electromagnetic field can have a profound impact on ourselves and the world around us. These studies have also shown that the heart can send signals to the brain through the vagus nerve, impacting cognitive processes and emotional regulation. Additionally, heart rate variability (HRV), which reflects the variation in time intervals between heartbeats, has been associated with various aspects of brain function, including attention, emotion regulation and cognitive performance.

So, doesn't the heart deserve the credit of cultivating joy, love and compassion in our lives?

In the end, while we may not be quite ready to swap out our thinking caps for thinking ventricles, we can certainly appreciate the whimsy of such a notion. So, the next time you are feeling stumped, just remember: Your heart might have the answers, or at the very least, it will keep pumping blood like a champ and helping you live whilst also managing the impact of cognitive processes and emotional regulations. Phew! that's no small feat for an organ that's just recently been promoted to head honcho!

It is worth mentioning that this phrase - *Heart is the New Brain* is not a widely recognized concept or scientific theory but is often used as a metaphorical expression in various contexts to emphasize the importance of emotions, intuition and empathy in our lives.

Don't you yet believe that embracing emotional intelligence, understanding our emotions and those of others, can lead to better decision-making, improved relationships and overall psychological well-being?

Significance Of Heart's Wisdom in A Digital Age

In a digital age, the concept of *heart's wisdom* takes on a new significance as we navigate the complexities and rapid changes of modern life. Here are a few ways to explore the heart's wisdom in a Digital Age:

1. **Mindfulness and Digital Well-Being:** With the constant influx of information and stimuli from digital devices, it is important to cultivate mindfulness and awareness of how these inputs affect our emotions and well-being. Practices such as meditation and deep breathing can help us reconnect with the wisdom of our hearts and maintain a healthy balance in the digital world.
2. **Compassionate Communication:** In the digital realm, communication often takes place through text, social media and other online platforms. It is important to remember the human element behind these digital interactions and to approach them with empathy, kindness and understanding. Communicating from the heart, even in a digital space, can foster genuine connections and meaningful relationships.

3. **Embracing Creativity:** The digital age offers countless opportunities for creative expression, whether through writing, art, music, or other forms of digital content. Engaging in a creative pursuit can be a powerful way to access the wisdom of the heart, express emotions and connect with others on a deeper level.
4. **Digital Detox:** Taking regular breaks from digital devices, disconnecting from screens at regular intervals even whilst at work, can provide an opportunity to reconnect with oneself and the world around us. By unplugging from technology, we create space for reflection, introspection and augment the cultivation of inner wisdom.
5. **Seeking Authentic Connections:** While social media and digital platforms can facilitate connections, they can also lead to superficial interactions and comparisons. It is important to seek out and nurture authentic connections with others, both online and offline, based on honesty, vulnerability and genuine human connection.

6. **Ethical Technology Use:** Being mindful of the impact of technology on ourselves and others is an important aspect of engaging with the digital world. This includes considering the ethical implications of our digital choices such as privacy, data security and the broader societal effects of technology.

By integrating these practices into our lives, we can tap into the wisdom of the heart and navigate the digital age with greater emotional intelligence, compassion and authenticity.

The statement "Heart is the New brain" is a metaphorical expression highlighting the significance of emotional intelligence, intuition in decision-making, empathy alongside rational thinking and overall human well-being aka personal growth. It emphasizes the idea that the heart, which symbolizes emotions and compassion, should play a significant role alongside the traditional notion of the brain, associated with logic and rationality.

In a society that often prioritizes the brain's rationality, recognizing the importance of emotions and intuition can lead to a more holistic and fulfilling life. Therefore, by incorporating the heart's wisdom, we can navigate the complexities of life with greater resilience and joy, tap into untapped potential, make more authentic decisions and deepen our connections with ourselves and others.

While there is ongoing research and discussion about the role of the heart in emotions, decision-making and overall well-being, it is important to note that the statement "heart is the new brain" is not a literal scientific finding. This metaphorical expression only suggests that emotional intelligence and intuition should be given equal importance alongside logical thinking and rationality.

Nevertheless, it is essential to approach this concept with critical thinking and consider multiple perspectives. The scientific understanding of the heart-brain connection is still evolving and further research is needed to fully understand the complexities of the heart-brain relationship.

Who needs a brain when your heart is the real mastermind!!

So, I am embracing the Heart's Wisdom,

Are You?

ACKNOWLEDGEMENT

A book such as this cannot be created by one or two people working alone. In fact, this one was improved immeasurably by the generous assistance of many talented people including my family, my colleagues, my friends. I am grateful to them all and deeply appreciative of the unswerving support I have received.

Finally, this book relies heavily on the real-life experiences of some of the world's most successful leaders. These men and women come from many disciplines, including business, academia, entertainment and government. They deserve much of the credit here.

Gratitude is all that I have in my Heart !!

www.ingramcontent.com/pod-product-compliance
Lightning Source LLC
LaVergne TN
LVHW012114160826
845678LV00014B/3082

9788197476105